Loss/Less

Rebecca A. Durham

Loss/Less

Rebecca A. Durham

Shanti Arts Publishing

Brunswick, Maine

LOSS/LESS

Published by Shanti Arts Publishing
Interior and cover design by Shanti Arts Designs

Cover image by Rebecca A. Durham, *Blue Alluvium*.
Acrylic on canvas. Used with the artist's permission.

Shanti Arts LLC
193 Hillside Road
Brunswick, Maine 04011
shantiarts.com

Printed in the United States of America

ISBN: 978-1-956056-16-7 (softcover)

Library of Congress Control Number: 2021951325

In memory of my father,
George Ingram Durham (1941-2020),
who gifted me love of nature and the art of noticing.

Contents

❖

AGGREGATIONS

This argillite is ripple lashed 12
Sky Prow Touches 13
Citizen of You, Penstemon 14
Look, your mind 15
Cloud Chords Considered 16
It's September & we 18
Petal Point 20
Ice Floes 21
Added Wolf Lichen 22
Whether or Not the Dark 23
Equinox 25
This Water Is Licked by Lambs 26
Flux Pulse 27
Inconsistent Stasis 28
O Fortuna This Dread Dark 31
Oblique Helix 32
Coextinction Cascade 34
Liquid with Incendiary Dignity 36
Why Can't I Stop Seeing Sparrow/Sorrow 37
Strip Mine 39
Viscosity 40
Stellate Pappus Never as Such 42
Human Impacts on Earth Systems in the
    Anthropocene: A Human/Other Narrative 45
Bird Count 51

❖

ARBOREAL BURIAL

[start with a tear] 54
[a lure of cerulean] 55
[gusseted obligations] 55
[oak branches] 56
[mountain brome] 56
[a twinged swale] 57
[larch needles rain] 58

[the ouzel on the log] 58

[blue stain fungus] 59

[when the light is red] 59

[grape fern spore rain] 60

[atmospheric fenestrations] 60

[the leaves] 61

[precarious cornice] 61

[just how far] 62

[build] 62

[dear chickadee] 63

[hot air under snow] 64

[larch shadows] 65

[juncos] 65

[crepuscular fenestrations] 66

[see life pulsing] 66

[hard to mouth] 67

[enduring her mystic face] 67

[in the morning] 68

[hello, the ocean was formal] 69

[inside a samara] 70

[unable to enable a quick] 70

[how else] 71

[wait a second wait a second] 71

[clear-cut] 73

[I sink my milk tooth] 73

[you are good enough] 74

[wanted to be porous] 74

[storm in the mountains] 75

[the emptyheads have forgotten] 75

[forgotten distinguished masters] 76

[sunset] 76

[this is how we kneel] 77

[reconcile with the forest] 77

[matter isn't excised or devised] 78

[this terrible distraction] 78

[trees & we] 78

Acknowledgements

Grateful acknowledgment is made to the editors of the following publications where poems first appeared:

Cold Mountain Review: "Coextinxtion Cascade," Spring/Summer 2019

Poetry Northwest: "Oblique Helix," Winter/Spring 2018

Humanities on the Brink: Energy, Environment, Emergency; A symposium sponsored by the Association for the Study of Literature and Environment (ASLE): "Bird Count" as "Bird Count: Avian Reverence/Violence Since Thoreau's Time at Walden," 2020

American Literature Association Conference, Thoreau Society Panel: "Bird Count" as "Bird Count: Avian Reverence/Violence Since Thoreau's Time at Walden," Boston, Massachusetts, 2021

AGGREGATIONS

This argillite is ripple lashed
time stamped by crests and dips

red waves in the forest
hot cliffs & heuchera

I'm walking in the mixed-con glade
through the cicada staccato

I catch a hint of bee-balm
intuit a faint sedge scent

desire affixes
like *Bryoria* on *Larix*

I hear an ever-waxing sound
grouse drum or thrush glissade

& you wanted to tether me
to those silent, colorless mediums

your shrill dark
loops don't slake me

in this rapt forest fervor
my storm roils arboreal

green needles
spindle up

hear the wildling wind
see the red sea thrashing

& I lashed
to her mast

Sky Prow Touches

treetops & never were such soundings

woven waves unraveling & illuminated goldenrod

scattered on hills & whirled with asters

when sparrows fledge the alders' green faith

spills the swarm & invents the whittled air & we

beside nominate the instant & gaze summon

the interior cobble & allow for the evolution of voices

furrowed colossal loess with toppled trunks as

though we sipped salient swells of pliant lilacs

& live to bloom like azure plum chandeliers & ask the

fireflies pinwheeling pulse sentience & light plus

a tempered dome of geometry of cliff gusts

gusseted by coils of crystals & testament of vaulted atolls

the cries of eagles & cathedrals of consequence

& all trivial mass impassive past the glass

Citizen of You, Penstemon

when I close my eyes
I see penstemon blue-violet

see cauline leaves
minutely hirtellous-puberulant

dust sticks to penstemon
to be buried /just
as of-part-of-the-pollen-record

all these genocided genomes
smothered in blue-violet

globose glands
glabrous ovary
glaucous leaves

o flagging earth, palette
of disappearing species
your worshipper
kneels in sight today

my last flag
waves corollas
blue-violet

rising from a caudex
rising from a caudex

this nation of one

Look, your mind
       follows bees to rose nectar
       finds red-tinged flares
       past where cleome falters

You are built from this distance
       appear in the vine-roofed hollow
       lattice of green planes
       where I stand unseen

Look at me with your mind
       I'm following a monarch across the garden
       she alights on coneflower, bee-balm, milkweed
       I shadow to find open wings

Look at me now across this distance, unseen
       I hold a branch of eastern larch
       fingers brush granite, mica flashes under ferns

You are speaking in the twilight slant light
       across swathes of green unbroken

I'm walking old sand and stone paths
       silt smells of life and mountains
       time is palpable over shifting matter
       deciduous flutter, chlorophyll flare

Look at me with your mind
       I'm sky-shaken
       cumulus clouds streak cerulean blues
         fern drenched fields
         red barns and granite steps

Cloud Chords Considered

vapor trill turning
still to brazen valence
angles of bluish elegance
scarlet sand malleable
metallic shadow equivalent
quavers lacustrine light tally
held by blue-green
algae sudden sugars
spun green from
rose chaos & globe
thistle trestles & hills
of celandine green
nether ether's water throat
ocular ice mist & lost
fumaroles' all-day seed
trees whisper & hemlock
trumpet leaf litter
fungal exalt frame
exit river & folded into
cotyledons on an etiolated
tongue & every marrow
our narrow feral hero & I
drink the river
from every side & each secret
a spring succor balance
of breached tumult ultimate
silver frost scribbled & the oiled
molt creased locus lotus
to us locked lilacs
sifting cell walls & gold
reticulate our lacquer
itself into errant iris & radiant
dissonance from afference
prism rhythm for the first

split trunk into illusion
cerulean stung leaves
lateral veins & green logos
accelerated ascent up the waves' sides
spoke ripples & breezy risers startling
starlings iridescent lift & ultramarine
martins imagine violet quartets
& invisible rootlets stem
from steepled status clouds & cupped
crags against the agate
intonation of particulate lapse & palpably
silken at most not a mountain
lichen orion milk moon & honed
drips apex sparks apart & grassy
lucid granite gowns resurrected
surreal & chiseled star static somber
equilibrium's penumbra to put
to use the pale realm of disjunct
jade seeps & vast dust
slips into ornate currents
hems the riparian expanse
aqueous chords crest over
land of mitotic millions &
centromeres mere halos

It's September & we

are primed
for decay's
reticent elegance

fall lures lingering blooms
goldenrod, yampah, sage
still green-blue
& summer stung

the sun's angle
deepens
rains crisp rays
over us

forests, hushed
by migration, wine-stained
with ninebark, clutch the last
of summer's colors

bud scales encircle us
mask nascent chloroplasts
so raw they'll glow green
with spring's pulse

we are latent fruit
entwined vines
we sense impending flight
& magnetism

fall mouths
fervor's caesura
taps the press
of longing

we do not speak
of verdure
or senescence
in these rain-scoured days

droplets beat onto
hollowing culms
conduct the hum
of what follows

remembering the heat
we linger by the river
watch water
knead light

Petal Point

politicians swarm like a mass of misfolded proteins
they dissolve less than half of what matters
and don't have everything to do with this
myelin sheaths are crumbling but forget all that
slogans slither from fists and vibe on tonal textures
larches are running on their own merits
their pitch is an echo of stones
they pivot the petal point, up high this time
out here where the fascicles thin
no longer bystanders
dark-eyed juncos are up for reelection
pollsters are knocking, looking for opinions
we're out here tapping maples, licking bark

Ice Floes

so easy to reach closer   touch the river   in the
tide of night   beyond patterned hills   twilight
twinged   silted shores almost pelagic   tracing
wider and wider arcs   circumboreal motion
ripples in the argillite
    migration of light   reach towards a smear of
stars   the Pleiades   this is how it unfolds
how stone features cloak the escarpment
    the path is strewn with percurrents   now it is
the angle of incidence
       sorting and separating this   metallic swish of
anabolism   shaping us like the river   hands
collecting silence
    ice floes moving over scales   ichthyologic
ampersands   enlivened by the cold   impervious
to impermanence   aphotic nights
  the ice thickening   a taste
of wintergreen   shaken from memory   myelination
offering this   through these   waves beyond
    the eventide   knowing what
the stones know   gathering
      what is ungathered

Added Wolf Lichen

Letharia vulpina

seeded Rocky Mountain bee plant
placed
   (((the pouring stone ( )   )))

one small monolith
miniature of the front pillar

((flourish when adored
nurture what has nurtured us))

green garden gods
garden only in tending

larch needles
the remainder
a reminder

forest
cultivated
like spirit fodder

this heterogeneousness
this wildling thing

Whether or Not the Dark

waxed & thick-walled
hyaline perfusion
this true guttural grasp
battled by threads

terpenoids or terpenes
culled compounds of interest
remedies from the roots
distilled by roseate dusk's

dense burdens
coalesced, synchronous
chronic anachronism, honest schism
a prism of honeyed prayers

the very same hues soothe
fluidity dictates this lustrousness
as the synapse slips & we who are nothing
the transient, tensile, our

cell walls leak porosity
osmotic insistence, a breach of solutes
& upon us quartzite veinlets of green, discrete
scattered grains, what's passed, what's past

water orbs on leaves fat like mercury
sun glinting in the hemlocks
author of lifelessness or direct duress
& say she sees the universe whole

monstrous & flung back
lousy chaos chooses looseness
keeps flicking the sky black
lack breaks her first loss

the false grass fesses first
her glance gleans lanced light
covets doves & dark coves
she wrests wrists from form

gallows of hung hellebore
bead lily lifting, a falter
spires weep or she weeps over
flayed layers of lignin

green gasps of bitter water
melancholic spruces
induction of the wry crescent
dicot tones born of burns

frayed layers of serrated skin
teal bleats to abate the scurried cyme
she believes in brined shadows
epithelial cells, arterial behind the blind

Equinox

nobody roots for us
save an astringent sun
that reflects vast and away
toward a tarnished field

regardless, I induce
the transition to elation
that polished emotion
shunned by barking men
with withered intellect

leaves morph from green to yellow
a variegation of ribs and veins
branches cultivate sparseness

autumn days condense
to mere light and motion
I hear the golden hymn
of gravity's cauldron

now I articulate
a blue-grey sky
fettered by none

I am an alchemist of the absolute
I paint the trees' tatters

This Water Is Licked by Lambs

if light is a mere imposter
    then water brims buoyant
        is a solvent of twilight

some water waits submerged
    but this water is aerated & underrated
        is almost as good as it used to be

recently this water was a clotted cloud
    this water has a killer attitude
        falls with altitude

this water tears through reluctant sediment
    saunters across the tarmac
        & pulses like iambs

this water frolics with hemlocks
    ferries fern spores from forests
        reflects phosphorescence & inflorescence

this water is a ceaseless torrent
    this water is a turbulent ebullience
        & an insurmountable mountain

      this water   is tainted with tar
is   bent   with   effluent
          this water   carries
      carcinogens
this water   warns us
      from an   oblique   queue
   this water   asks us   to query excess
       this water   chokes
     on   our
    viscous silence

Flux Pulse

the common feeling, free of fixity, unshadowed, mouths of sunken clouds, dagger of ether that cleaves you from my sight, extravagant wind-sculpted sand, stiff sodden with stillness, ephemeral ruffles, lacerated peaks and gullies, alleviation of the illumed, churn of rain brushing against the canopy of entropy, innumerable billow, futility of fixity, time reeling with reciprocity, potent flux pulse, piqued by the scrutiny of complexity, dredging the recumbent torrent, wake of breath, vinous chorus, intermittent watercourse, ink petal bells, peels from the internal inflorescence, discs filled with proboscises and fits of sugar, sky sweet, nectar suspended and carried off by desire, burbling on into the wing hum, how's that, how's that, tufts of witness, concord of fern fronds, green amulets, the ordinary certainty of cessation, simultaneous tumult, tensile tug of telos, this heron feeling, torqued willow, stark swallow, sedge spread, cedars silent astride, entire pillars, relinquished glass crash, oblique anguish, dilated pearl ponds, shells harnessed by somnolence, intervals of intrigue, threads of violet trust, the old shiver of surrender, bright point of persistent haunts, palm of sand, grain of hand, practical rapture, precision of erose insight, sought by bliss, incredulous nacreous night, hush of half-articulate touch, astir with the whirr of tortured matter, extinct tinctures, impartial partitions, distinguished by love or anguish or lack of lily-light, leaves of ordinary arguments, gaunt thoughts, unanimous animation, mineral gilt, flank of basalt, rudder of rock, current of chalcedony, faces of plagioclase, feldspar sparks, siliceous spaciousness, tenuousness, slip our hands to twine, enter a ripple, aggregation of gather, sharp-edged sedges slip in, thread crimson fragments, absorb the opposite instinct, tepals in our spines, rivers opening, adhere adhere adhere, a stability now yields, billows a guttural utterance, clutch of measureless abundance, sentient sounds, immersed in precise pressure, sway of simultaneity, electron envy, quixotic crickets mock twilight's torpor, sound canters over fraying hills, disembodies darkness, rivers winnow contours, snow spindles into hemlock lakes, storm surge, then sudden sun, violet light, sandstone tones coo the aria of morning, open our fluviatile throats to spout the fugue, cohere cohere cohere

Inconsistent Stasis

I

luminous with illusion
an illation begins
lures us to the distillate
with unrivaled devotion

fragmentation as absorption
we echolocate to orient the finite
engage in this act of finding
blue and translucent

II

unnatural aberration
they forget the smell of sedges
heady black muck
organic saturation

water licks the green shards
licks brown culms
when time is repealed
florets will flow unfettered

III

sometimes roots never loosen
sometimes a butterfly is a fulcrum
see this dark smudge
or surge of urgency

we never saw it coming
stood at the edge of shatter
should have seen it coming
crooked and bedraggled

IV

at the fringes writhes
the derivation of violet
this silver violence
forged from forget

V

what makes us buoyant
not the squeeze of evening
nor the innumerable compendium
of an indigo aperture

VI

stasis spurs equilibrium
reciprocal integration
we hug our small realities
retire to the flowerfields

VII

it was a false summit
we surmised
the broken basalt
an alloy of the absolute

take these cottonwood bones
or the miracle of cotyledons
the struggle of reeds and ferns
this cessation of friction

VIII

we hear a summons among leaves
cytokines and lipid layers
a tangle of molecules
lurch of detritus

take these aggregations of atoms
folded and misfolded
differentiation always explicit
what they feel and how they speak

O Fortuna This Dread Dark

sleepless excess
hollow hole, falling, yet you say

                                    release the chasm's clutch
                                    soften the grip of the lariat

                                    can you see the bee-balm
                                    honeycombed involucres
                                    fruit cusps spent and withering
                                    how she sings, yet her matter's
                                            a mere integer
                                    eeking out a finite form
                                            in a steady state
                                    of continuous numbers

                                    accede her continuousness
                                    her integrity, energetically

                                            breathe
                                            with her

                                    the thin arch moon mines for light
                                    leaves skate the street
                                    stars wade through satellites, smog
                                    to arrive here, here now, to brighten you

                                            arrive
                                    in the night-stung light

motion invades viscosity
slicks electrons to spin

        a pastness, a pastness

        so tender that torment
                of apart

Oblique Helix

] I [have become impermeable
gated by ligands

                                        conductive to sound only
                                     somewhere in the continuum
                    I sense   [god] not your god not the one
                                         of religion or
                 matter
                                              or anything except
irradiated energy

      flood the K+/Ca+ channels
                                I am responsive to current
                                             ] responsive [

voltage varies
         opens or shuts the gate [

                          unleash the cellular lasso

invert this
                                       ] open [
                                             this amplitude

I slip   through the gating ring

           I'm the [
                          I] sense
                                        excitatory subunits [I'm]
              hyper-polarized

                          [I spark the gates

the sky writhes in me
pull away lungs   to feel/fill my heart with blood

    between systole/diastole is the flare of me

              [such a lush threshold, flesh]

Coextinction Cascade

keywords: food webs; mutualistic networks;
network motifs; coextinction

great auk, flightless
com-p+le-x eco+logi_cal_net-work
rate and shape of which
therefore, loss

the disassembly of ecological networks
leads to thresholds whereupon the network
      co+l)lapses
                    habitat
razed/erased, last seen [ ]
biased pruning of the t[r/ee of l}/if/e
Darwin's fox, umbrella species
                    fr+agility
Global change
is one of the leading problems
faced by h_u_&m/an/[kind]

roughly speaking, let us imagine
Bornean orangutan, teetering
so far we can speak only of

there is still a large gap
in our un_d_er{st_and[_)ing
of this problem

in order to assess, perhaps also relates
                  more pronounced loss
ili pika
nature of the [co]ex_t/in(ct/i)on cascade
these very preliminary results
on both the assembly of ecological networks

and its collapse after perturbations
informed extinction model
robustness   of
          of   sudden collapse
suddenly \e%a{\r_th\ felt less cohesive

The reader should recognize, however,
that this knowledge is still
very f{r=ag}_ment[[]e/d

Liquid with Incendiary Dignity

water laps the shore of vision
senses carve delineations

the bog flickers with false cinders
cotton grass lies lush with fog

this friction inflects the rising river
culms cantilever over green

I'm leaning over the edge where
leaked salt falls like a lasso

the leaves & I resist
the opaque queues

time with its barnacle shards
bleeds purpled pearl

no one taught me how to twine a chasm's tendrils
or that efflorescence is the ghost of gravity

I reach into the wet abyss
quake the very sedge that cuts me
it culls the thought fire & scarifies my skin

I appreciate this kind of ecstasy

I hold a needle to the stomatic swell
rise from the swamp-wet silt

Why Can't I Stop Seeing Sparrow/Sorrow

I saw it molten
this body between takes
never diminished
in the folds of silence
see us as an assemblage
some vast room post-collapse
the machine that exceeds itself
summons us from excess
suppose the body suppose
I saw it stolen

❖

craved vacancy, crooked verity
we summon the imminent crescendo
gravity, ineptitude
mottled meter split with loss
I heard wind bottom out into spacelessness
reflection of fierceness
thuddy & direct

❖

an indigo surge
greedy integers garner light
take us to the other side of grief
a wet iridescence
teases fractals from futility
a bundle of culms, factual atoms
we mouth off to fraught ecology

a pulse of plastic
what carries us downstream
carries us crumpled
detritus & dust, gussets of trash
the remainder equals a function of
I dive for it, want to save it
I thought I heard an asking
going round & round the eddy

❖

birdsong had bustled
why can't we hear it anymore
when I turn the corner of shadow
I leak ultramarine blue
I plead with us to listen
inequity a fast fall from symmetry
such a surprise at this late hour
we walk through edges we can't discern
brush them with our moth wings

❖

there are riffles here
somewhere spit-soaked & certain
the river surges with indifference
crosses dissonance until it intersects
with duress why is it called white noise
what if noise is gray or if disarray
is a prism of disembodied darkness
I want to untangle this sparrow
the riff of white at her throat
noiseless now in the roil

Strip Mine

unfettered mind, liquid mind, anemochorous mind, mind with
barbed achenes arcing over fields and plucked by fickle hands, mind
swiped left and right, mind bobbling, mind a granite erratic shook
by mass wasting, mind caught in contrails of bigot planes, mind
dragged behind and tear-stained, mind as marigold flower of the dead,
mind placated, mind riddled with plaques, mind congealment of
concealments, mind minted with collector coins, mind a bitcoin mine
the tipping point of our catastrophe, mind the last migrating monarch,
mind oozing milkweed, mind dehiscent, mind derivative, mind this
harsh mine

Viscosity

the surface beckons—
reflections illuminate
one strand of sky
we covet as blue

I / you see it—
we are riveted
riven

synapses track and recreate
geometry, physics
the electron roil

matter, even pulsing—
the pause of approximation
between expectation and motion

we watch it cease
to be a seam
between self/ Self/ us

we cease to be anything
but sky-dust

now lucid color—
time folds through itself

to drink this ice age residual
to touch this mercurial mirage
        we are oscillating cinders
        slick with life

atoms helix light
quiver like silver

we seine waves
parse sky slivers

now nothing retains
the taint of apart—
neither matter
nor water

Stellate Pappus Never as Such

natural springiness that binds them
that thrive there

that spun from
o holy colony cellulose drawn

save zero vine veins & barb coils
[magnification unknown]

multiples of fours, threes, twos
or single furrow [absence of insects]

swollen roots tree rings [nourish]
certain cacophony enables beheld

what deeds castaway blaze
lost continent sequence [consequence]

field frame kaleidoscope myth maze
[we listen for] hallelujahs & floods

the final flesh muse mesh [enkindled]
lodestar [magnification unknown] wake

pulse quest unhinged void the universe
pluriverse what scorches uproar

[our umbilicus] under us
weigh the whole vast extinction

expanse of bled thunder dust plumbed
from circumference & snared trust lifts us

into whirled stance immanent mind
& innate seeds congregate pigment

congruent with plain signs elemental
angles terrestrial torsion & farther out

from peddled death cast unto detritus
drawn by plow shell shadows & abalone

coils noise of arms folded into fabled bones
lucidity of lineament [from whose dust]

we mention what's among us to sing
a name obsidian or lapis our lips become

stone again & incandescent truths gust from
waterfalls & evolution of starry perches punctuated

by death dread pressed into cell wall margins
[our origins] feats of edifice stern dreams immense

rifts aloft [surround succumb] continuum of dawn
smelter of sight [however you ignite it] reveal

resplendent cobbled banner agape with osmosis
& a mockery of sunshine leads us to the avalanche

an apogee of doubt hails the nested quest & a quicksand
catches quavering ravens inking forests

knit by dusk [who stares air] receding clear
into antipodes & wisp green lake summit this

ecstasy of veiled woods & geodesic atoms of attainment
[distant: magnification unknown] keeled deeds imagine

the pendant planets & immeasurable ebb threads wanes
the whirls boundless catalyst & the base of bottomless

[no matter the furl] was not this way [embroidered by order]
splintered angles hanging by sliding lines & unhewn hereafter

elderberry's grey-blue berries take the ionic descent
or elegiac gain of light across basalt impermanence

& azimuth of periphery or eternity spheres of pierced universe
leaking cobalt circuity & this threshold of immense immanence

magnification unknown

Human Impacts on Earth Systems in the Anthropocene: A Human/Other Narrative

Abstract

someone says
STOP, Being—

& here
we kneel

Introduction

first we gave each other our gazes
the fawn without moving wasn't there
I averted   became wide berth
was anti-disturbance she/we   unwary   aware

lichens leak from fingers/vision   crush color
we're epiphytes   we're unable to resist *being*
when I come to rest   larches   become we

these forests
        aren't *productive*
we're unproductive   with them
                                we are radical in bentness
we are overstocked thicket   mistletoe topiary
we are (thrushes) singing   swallowtails unfurl & I   follow

we walk wide berths
skirt pre-emergent herbicide they say *instant re-entry* say
non-toxic but a smell says

$$\text{\textit{something else}}$$

says   wide berth   says
          someone will soon stop being there

I gather my being   here   aren't *productive*   become

an aversion
          to green growing   brown dread as we await   machines
to *fix the forests*   fix *productivity*   thrush babies   unaware
wary   we're blind still   no wide berth   we
want to say STOP   thrush sings
stop, beings   & together
                  we're watching

Materials & Methods

Coyote first wild of the day, not even out of the truck, ochre flash
of tail loping away. Down the sharp slope toward the light green on
the aerial, can only mean wetland. I seek the aberrations, survey the
anomalies. Down the old skid trail over slash & sticks, steep enough
to slip on moss & I fall before finding a couple stout sticks to temper
my descent. Toward the draw & I'm drawn like the Swainson's
thrush who I hear down there spiraling song through the thicket.
Past the second-growth firs & choke of ninebark until I hear water
& see nothing but a swath of close green. Western birch & Rocky
Mountain maple & mock orange block the flow but I hear it even
over the thrushes who surround me now, invisible in the deep green
branches. Through the currants & rose & hawthorn until I am in

it, the wet seep of cool mud cresting my boots & the monkeyflower poised over the slow creek like pursed yellow lips. Too slow to drink, water widens here into a fragrant spread of muck & life & pools & seeps. I find grape fern, a squeal-worthy new addition to our plant list, run my fingers over the sporophyte. This marks the depth of richness, the dark black soil so full it lured this fern ally. I follow the water to the boundary where it fans out into a spring-fed spread where insects flock. To understand that water is life is to squat here in the hum & flutter. I watch the wing dance until the heat bakes my back & head to the animal path near the water that wends in the near-closed canopy. Upstream, returning now & then to crawl through the dense shrubs to not miss anything, thorns scrape my skin & sticks lodge in my hair & I claw & wade through what the water brings. Back on the path I startle a snake who disappears under an alder bole. Almost where the water is underground I stop among the chickadees, *dee-dee-dee* they scold, curious & then fly close. I talk back, make my best impression of the burrs & dees & now there are ten of them, excited, coming closer & looking & scolding, although one of them approves of me & maybe thinks of taking a chance, starts the *fee-bee* call, which I always think of as *love-me* & I do love back though they might be saying *get the hell outta here* or maybe just *who ARE you*. A scarlet tanager also comes to cluck & scold, cardinal-red head & warbler-yellow body blazing from the dull brown branches. I call to them & call to them & they surround me for ten minutes or so until the heat feels acute & I'm out of water so I walk upslope until all signs of water are gone & the heat captures all sound except the insect swell of chitin & wings. This is how I enter the forest & this it how it enters me too, in increments, following the water of our bodies until we become our own wet ecology, integrated & held.

Results

katydid   katydid   katydid   katydid   katy   katydidn't   katy   katydid
katydid   katydid   katydid   katydid   katydid   katydid   katydid
katydid   katydid   katydid   katydid   katydid   katy   katydid   katydid
katydid   katydid   katydid   katydid   katy
katydid   katydid   katydid   katydid   katydidn't   katydid   katy   katy
katydid   katydid   katydid   katydidn't   katy   katydid   katy
katydid   katydid   katy   katydidn't   katydid   katydid   katydid   katy
katydid   katy   katydid   katydid   katydid   katydid   katydid
katydid   katydid   katydid   katydid   katydid
katy   katydid   katydid   katydid   katydid   katydidn't   katydid
katydid   katydid   katydid   katydid   katydid   katydidn't   katydid
katydid   katy   katydid   katy   katydid   katydid   katydidn't
katydid   katydid   katydid   katy   katydid   katy   katydid
katydid   katydidn't   katydid   katydid   katydid   katydid
katy   katydid   katy   katydid   katydid   katydid   katydidn't
katydid   katydid   katydid   katydid   katydid   katy   katydid
katy   katydidn't   katydid   katydid   katydid   katydid
katydid   katydidn't   katydid   katydid   katydid   katy   katydid
katy   katydid   katydid   katydid   katy   katydidn't   katydid
katydid   katydid   katydid   katydid   katydidn't   katydid
katydid   katydid   katydid   katy   katydid   katy   katydid
katydidn't   katy   katydid   katy   katydid   katydid   katydid
katydid   katydid   katydidn't   katydid   katydid   katy   katydid
katy   katydid   katy   katydid   katy   katydid   katydid
katydidn't   katydid   katydid   katy   katy   katydid   katy   katydid
katy   katydid   katydid   katydid   katydidn't   katydid   katydid
katy   katydid   katy   katydid   katy   katydid   katy   katydid
katydid   katydidn't   katydid   katydid   katydid   katykatydid
katy   katydid   katydid   katydidn't   katydid   katy   katydid
katy   katydid   katydid   katydid   katydid   katydidn't   katydid
katydid   katy   katydid   katy   katy   katydid   katydid   katydid
katy   katydid   katydidn't   katydid   katydid   katydid   katydid
katydid   katydid   katydid   katydid   katydid   katy   katydid
katy   katydid   katy   katydid   katy   katydid   katydidn't

katydid katydid   katydid   katydid   katydid   katydidn't
katydid katydid   katydid   katydid   katydid   katy   katydid
katy   katydidn't   katydid katydid   katydid   katydid katydid
katydidn't   katydid katydid   katydid   katydid   katydid
katydidn't   katydid katydid   katydid   katy   katydid katy
katydid   katydid   katydidn't   katydid katydid   katydid   katy
katydid katy   katy   katydid katy   katydid   katy   katydid
katy   katydid   katydidn't   katydid katydid   katydid   katydid
katydid   katydid   katydid   katydid katydidn't   katydid katydid
katydid   katydid   katydid   katydidn't   katydid katydid
katy   katydid katy   katydid   katydid   katydid   katy   katydid
katy   katydidn't   katydid katydid   katydid   katy   katydid
katy   katydid   katydid   katydidn't   katydid katy   katydid
katy   katydid   katydid   katydid   katydid   katydid katydid
katydid   katydidn't   katydid katy   katydid katy   katydid   katy
katydid katy   katydid   katydid   katydid katy   katydid katy
katydidn't   katydid katydid   katy   katydid katy   katydid
katydid   katydid   katydidn't   katydid katydid   katydid
katydid   katydid   katydidn't   katydid katydid   katydid
katydid   katy   katydid katy   katydid   katydid   katydid katydid
katydidn't   katydid katydid   katydid

Discussion

dark lily sobs for extant or extinct
our garden mirrors a swarm of sunset littered
with 2-diethylhyroxymethylbenzene
or is it Diethyl (hydroxymethyl)phosphonate
$HOCH_2P(O)(OC_2H_5)_2$ no I mean toxin
tell me what is the isomer of grief because
pebbled with intention I inspect the tender wonders
I stop water falling & om with spreading fingers

droplets fling & cave over air like epithelial cells
metastasis should be a good word as in mega stasis
equilibrium but scars make a certain kind of kindling
memory bears the fruit of shadow & bright haunt makes a fever of it
with geometric pressure becomes the solemn molecule
this is how it breaks
methane spews over amber waves or in amber waves
marica marica a marica what did you do to apoptosis
what was placid is elastic or plastic or caustic
cuts light into parcels & delivers them by drone
holds a ladder to an iris to watch the gaze of night blur
because faint delicate breath
& because mysterious symbiosis
the history of extraction became prophecy
carcinogenic snow spills a hydrocarbon creation story
this is how we break
I call a moratorium on cement or at least errant elements
I can taste the vacancy of extinction
I am asking what is our ecstasy in acquisition
this is an inquisition into our monstrous lust
the river was sheer eyed & eloquent in its entirety
I knelt there with blue praise in bruised pines
I knelt there making a fever of it

Conclusion

acorn,
the good news is greenness

Bird Count

for Henry David Thoreau

Henry when I listen for *Strix varia* sometimes I hear someone crying. I look up for wings and I see a man draped in a rainbow chute spiraling down the thermals.

Henry when I heard the barred owls on that North Fork ridge I felt whole again. Now I hear the droll hum of the highway's auditory effluent. Low whirr machine wind. A chickadee flitting in between the heavy beaking of Eurasian sparrows.

Henry I hear the eastern blue jay out here in the west.

Henry I saw the dipper dip deeper than ever & spill into tainted ether.

Henry you said nothing could defile this pond. You said so many things.

Henry I know that you saw god out there. Nature bloomed in your hand—when you reached through yourself to shake hands with heaven—cast in a green pond's eye.

Henry, did you lie to me? Henry *Strix varia, Strix varia, Strix varia. Strix varia* in the spruces, the great fluviatile gather.

The loon graces you, Henry, *Gavia immer.*

Henry I sit here in the backyard to notice—ponds are hard to come by these days—and study the new larches' needle count. Only new growth from the season now spins gold. I hear *faint silvery warblings.*

Henry you wouldn't want it this way. I drink from rivers that poison me, just to quench my thirst.

Henry— ethereal spiral
I love the hermit thrush too

ARBOREAL BURIAL

start with a tear
an incision

a mockery of trees' effrontery
bark & lichen guts
spilled on the forest floor

there is a will submerged
encrusted with dust

a pattern of utterance
constrained in history

without distress or qualification
customary manifestation

unnerved by dazzling ecologies
minds deform ideas
of what should be

the previous expansive splendor
not disrespected
but not untouched

flare of a dragonfly
an iridescence
that broke shadow

I imagined us there
imagined persistent wilderness

a realm of water not brackish
not fracked

I'm not sure if anybody was there

❖

a lure of cerulean
concerns itself with symbols
centrally sought

wrought sound
contrasts directly
with simulated smoothness

these mossy accomplishments
seem natural

the high sheen of cell walls
holds orbs of water

a hum of understanding
brims warm

❖

gusseted obligations

we scour our illusions
onto river gravel

vestiges of gesture

unresolved solvents
drip from unevolved evolution

give way to ultraviolet vigilance
revolved volition

call it insect wings
call it crank & flutter

the cadence of trauma
or lucidity of budscales

❖

oak branches
delineate the diurnal

at night the mind queries
silhouettes of star shards

a box elder bug in the cathedral
autumn's holy torpor

torrents of leaves
gaunt flight, the eternal plummet

can't stop inking
the equations

migrating passerines spiral
into the light cone of the 9/11 memorial

until someone calls
& says turn off the light

❖

mountain brome
waves to coalesced senses

striations over sand

iterations of hematite

shifting lips

❖

a twinged swale
fluorite, labradorite, agate

the old exalted quiet
like the desert on a windless day

no susses in the creosote
no matter shifting about

sitting on the bole of the green ash
head against the deep grey furrows

dried leaves clicking
against each other

no one expects you
to be huddled up
to wooden towers
or buried in furrows

cathedral bells call out
some tenuous nuance

it's late says the furrow
it's late says the twisted bark
it's late says the waxwing beaking berries

serrated ash leaves
tinge yellow & inroll

❖

larch needles rain

spin parallel to the lake
spin end to end

the same paralellity
all the way down

now I know how you plummet

❖

the ouzel on the log
over the shallow outlet
knee dips & darts

I don't bother her

moths lose their sense of sky
or gravity is reflexive
or magnetic inclination is rhetorical

either way the lake surface is raised
with moth bodies

& I gawk in the womb lull
with no hard ground, hard choices
or hard grief

this grand gold larch
this northerly mother

continual presence
scaffolding

chromatic influx

don't waste it

❖

blue stain fungus
sidewinder serendipity

they think they have to manage
while I have been asleep

cerulean blue fluidity
leave room for the water

red-winged blackbird on lush cattail
meadowlark on bitterbrush
hermit thrush or varied thrush or
Swainson's thrush, keep recalling

leave room for the water

the will of furrows
obsidian between fronds

productivity vs. effulgent verdure

roundabout with beargrass
roundabout with buffaloberry

❖

when the light is red
all I see is blue

snow crystals on the tongue
a taste of winter
waning color

larch needles
on yellow-gold ground

opulent immanent
needle rain

now haven, now home

❖

grape fern spore rain

elegant green tongues
grey-green & holding

hard frost
cracks cell walls

aster petals
licked with ice

❖

atmospheric fenestrations
reluctant heat, tentative light

cold wilt & pumpkins
pawed by does

ice glints
on port-red orbs

only half the branches
are illuminated

the other half follow
the dichotomy

complete the whole

❖

the leaves
on my avenue
aren't flying

the moon
must be
waxing

❖

precarious cornice

black shadows under the dock

roadkill mottled & disheveled

firs fat with mistletoe

dark of the second peak back

fog foraging for shadows

spectacle of branches

disturbed river

moon's deepest visible crevasse

morning star in the planets' elliptic

lacustrine trust

haggard mallards

❖

just how far
wends your wood-wide-web

imagine mycelial mats

imagine solutes traveling earthward

through cambium
then horizontal through soil
& back up again

we are surge of micronutrients
we wonder if our voice is hydrophilic
we wonder about our molecular weight

we swear we hear your groans

❖

build
sandcastles of the body
in low tide

every night erases

don't recognize
the shag of skin

rime coats all roughness
everything congruent with ice

level with the understory
earth-death-melancholia
hardens like paste

clutch the larch as if forget
how to unclench

you are a little white dot
seen from Mars

we are a little white dot
seen from anywhere

hugging the same space
trees squeezed whole

❖

dear chickadee
you are the object of my politics

dear larch
you are the object of my politics

dear death of life
none of which were ever objects

mouthless, pulverized, unlearned

we reorient our alular wings

fringed mushroom unfurls
        eloquent   whorls

calls us back to closeness

   you must have missed me
all night   you tried
        to make a nest
            with my body

scatter sunflower seeds
over snow-crusted raised beds

when the juncos come
they fill us
with the fitted particulars

integral in their fervor
gradual in their myth

❖

hot air under snow
subnivean zone

xenocryst: catalyst
amethyst: henotheist

sap that writhes
finds its way
from my throat

clutch the larch & whisper
tell your treople I love you

bark licker!
tastes of snow & sap

bark hugger!
arms that reach find fullness

❖

larch shadows
engulf us

we tuck tight
into deciduousness

early earnest kiss
fistful of falling lichen

did we
        gather wood
gather other-ether

how we came to know ourselves
in relation to the turning

a long orange band of sound
irruptive & imperceptible

save with mycelium ears

❖

juncos
are wintering here

◈

crepuscular fenestrations
climate rage
disarray

habitability instability
a shrinking

insistent accelerant
a carbon bargain

take this little dot
& squeeze

take the platelets
& empty cells

bioaccumulation
of toxic smog

burnt anthropogenic VOC's
the needles know your name

needles know
our reference condition

◈

see life pulsing
in the little white dot

what if we look like
purple loosestrife

nothing differentiated
we must be hard to mouth

❖

hard to mouth
our blindness manifesto

ragged branches of
split peg lichen

easily parsable, or related
either none of them
or all of them

resurrect
the extinct

tell your treople
I didn't want it
to be this way

tell your treople
I'm sorry

❖

enduring her mystic face
her terrible benign power

work the obsidian
point chip rock

fever smooth
depressions & pits

coming over the brow
of the range

a shallow root
a tree's birth

trembling spring

❖

in the morning
also in motion

collapse

in the morning
collapse

also in motion
awakening

morning
in the
   morning
splinters
spike my thighs

clear-cuts
lodge my torso

pluck out the bone

was I pulped
was I loved
was I wasted

when I die
extinct trees
will come for me

sunken faith

❖

hello, the ocean was formal

neither swaying of wolf bay
        nor slaying of the bay

touch the estuary
        make a high road
        broken & taken

fern fronds always outside
        scrubbing smokestacks

sitting on forced feet
        reminded of streaming
        reminded of water

it was to be expected
        not spoken

the sound of waxwings
        before overrun with plainness
        before drone of ruin

forces few new news
        save
exploitation exaltation

❖

inside a samara
happy harbinger
of flight

first latch a cache of craters
cloud moat of water

I ought to swim farther
in cold enfolded

with whom do I converse
about filaments of lichens
strewn between larch nodes

I nod to nobody
sunrise has the forest haunted

a kaleidoscope of complexity
saskatoon's ephemeral bloom

any lack anymore
implore the celestial system

if possible or audible

❖

unable to enable a quick
nutrient sink or transpiration blink

waxwings mouth ash
eye corymbose elderberry

elusive loops loose shape

erose edges
flank the staunch branch

red rings collapse on cattails
mud jolts from a curl of soil

moss smothers a cradle of argillite
sun-split fissures of sheer splendor

wine red ninebark wanes
because crisp diagonals

because teeth frayed fescue
because create something

matter never created nor destroyed
but divvy up light in fractals &

can smell broken linkages
the double helices

❖

how else
can the woodland
woo us

❖

wait a second wait a second
just wait

axles & cutters & shredders
are coming

my life breath
is caught in your throat

shyness of shyness
brings the branches to near touching

in the space between
restless stones pre-date us

step up into it
realms of bliss or blackness or green

frustrated strangeness
earth death

mineral soul/soil
wait

don

       active soaring wings
       passive soaring wings
       elliptical wings
       high speed wings
       hovering wings

none of these
were plucked

my primary feathers
secondary, coverts, alula
marginal & scapular

entangled in the wreck
their open palm madness

❖

clear-cut

sick empty

whether eyes closed or open

a haunting

❖

I sink my milk tooth
into the hollow egg of disaster

rare things grow
when I'm trying

wetlands

horsetail skullcap mint
facultative wetland plants

existence of pre-existence
unfamiliar

a wet suck of peat
forgotten birds

forgotten blossoms
insects at the gate

insects
click of beetle wings

spurious landscape
furious & extinct

I see a dew-laden web
the pattern revives me

what do you call the unknowing
do you call it god

❖

you are good enough
we take it all back

unscathe us

unblast
unleach
unmine
unslash unburn

uncut, uncut
uncut uncut uncut
uncut

all those holy trees

❖

wanted to be porous
so sparse, elemental

so as caste in the stream
will float like tuff

to be like chalcedony
or chert

smooth with sharp edges
showing

cool basalt under the waterfall
flanked with wet ferns

intricate as a saxifrage
irregular carpals

now like diorite
in raven's shadow

trees work
their good in me

I gather bitter fruits
map my fissures

❖

storm in the mountains
feel the branches surge

untethered jettison
wild thrash

❖

the emptyheads have forgotten
they are forests

the emptyheads have forgotten
they are trees

❖

forgotten distinguished masters
brown creeper feeds skyward

in another year
concentric ring

another year
mindless felling

windfall of pulp
windfall of fracture

❖

sunset
of the golden season

fruits of the green gamble
germination of autumn annuals

we were drought stricken
dehiscent

cambium of chapped lips

no water
but the rush of leaves

we sip dew orbs
suckle sap

❖

this is how we kneel
at the altar of our alders
and listen to the towhee

this is how we kneel

this is how we kneel
at the hemlock

pulled back
from the brink

pulled back from the helm
of helplessness, hatred

nobody
at
that
helm
anymore

helm—>hemlock—>home

❖

reconcile with the forest:
        an integrated mind
        is a wordless mind

the yoked yearn
for nothing

snow in the larch branch

do the trees regret
letting me

❖

matter isn't excised or devised

or ever done with itself

we are an encircling torrent

we walk into the circuitous forest

trilliums intuit us

we elucidate nothing

we are illicitly complicit

in disaster

❖

this terrible distraction

no more trees here

no more trees there

what kind of extinction is this

❖

trees & we
share
a fifth of our genes

do they teach us
anything
de-civilized

they've studied us
find us simultaneous
find us
unearned & unlearned

they put their seeds in us
synthesized into genes

these molecules
of remembering

About the Author

photo credit: Emaline Aspen

Rebecca A. Durham is a poet, botanist, and artist. Originally from New England, she currently lives in Montana. Rebecca's writing has been featured in national and international journals, literary magazines, and anthologies. *Half-Life of Empathy*, an award-winning book of ecopoetry, was published in 2020 (New Rivers Press).

—www.rebeccadurham.net

SHANTI ARTS

NATURE ▪ ART ▪ SPIRIT

Please visit us online
to browse our entire book catalog,
including poetry collections and fiction,
books on travel, nature, healing, art,
photography, and more.

Also take a look at our highly regarded art
and literary journal, *Still Point Arts Quarterly*,
which may be downloaded for free.

www.shantiarts.com

www.ingramcontent.com/pod-product-compliance
Lightning Source LLC
Chambersburg PA
CBHW070814280326
41934CB00012B/3187